Sewing Log Book

INFORMATION

NAME

ADDRESS

E-MAIL ADDRESS

WEBSITE

PHONE   **FAX**

EMERGENCY CONTACT PERSON

PHONE   **FAX**

Sewing Log Book

DETAILS

PROJECT ....
CREATED FOR ....
DATE STARTED .... **DATE COMPLETED** ....
ITEM .... **QTY** ....
PRICE .... **DEPOSIT PAID** .... **BALANCE PAID** ....
PATTERN USED ....
SUPPLIES NEEDED ....

SKETCH / PHOTO

NOTES

....
....
....
....
....
....
....
....

Sewing Log Book

DETAILS

PROJECT ....

CREATED FOR ....

DATE STARTED .... DATE COMPLETED ....

ITEM .... QTY ....

PRICE .... DEPOSIT PAID .... BALANCE PAID ....

PATTERN USED ....

SUPPLIES NEEDED ....

SKETCH / PHOTO

NOTES

....
....
....
....
....
....
....
....

Sewing Log Book

DETAILS

PROJECT ....
CREATED FOR ....
DATE STARTED .... DATE COMPLETED ....
ITEM .... QTY ....
PRICE .... DEPOSIT PAID .... BALANCE PAID ....
PATTERN USED ....
SUPPLIES NEEDED ....

SKETCH / PHOTO

NOTES

....
....
....
....
....
....
....
....

Sewing Log Book

DETAILS

PROJECT ....
CREATED FOR ....
DATE STARTED .... **DATE COMPLETED** ....
ITEM .... **QTY** ....
PRICE .... **DEPOSIT PAID** .... **BALANCE PAID** ....
PATTERN USED ....
SUPPLIES NEEDED ....

SKETCH / PHOTO

NOTES

....
....
....
....
....
....
....
....

Sewing Log Book

DETAILS

PROJECT ....
CREATED FOR ....
DATE STARTED .... **DATE COMPLETED** ....
ITEM .... **QTY** ....
PRICE .... **DEPOSIT PAID** .... **BALANCE PAID** ....
PATTERN USED ....
SUPPLIES NEEDED ....

SKETCH / PHOTO

NOTES

....
....
....
....
....
....
....

Sewing Log Book

DETAILS

PROJECT ....
CREATED FOR ....
DATE STARTED .... DATE COMPLETED ....
ITEM .... QTY ....
PRICE .... DEPOSIT PAID .... BALANCE PAID ....
PATTERN USED ....
SUPPLIES NEEDED ....

SKETCH / PHOTO

NOTES

....
....
....
....
....
....
....
....

Sewing Log Book

DETAILS

PROJECT ....

CREATED FOR ....

DATE STARTED .... **DATE COMPLETED** ....

ITEM .... **QTY** ....

PRICE .... **DEPOSIT PAID** .... **BALANCE PAID** ....

PATTERN USED ....

SUPPLIES NEEDED ....

SKETCH / PHOTO

NOTES

....
....
....
....
....
....
....

Sewing Log Book

DETAILS

PROJECT ....
CREATED FOR ....
DATE STARTED .... DATE COMPLETED ....
ITEM .... QTY ....
PRICE .... DEPOSIT PAID .... BALANCE PAID ....
PATTERN USED ....
SUPPLIES NEEDED ....

SKETCH / PHOTO

NOTES

....
....
....
....
....
....
....

Sewing Log Book

DETAILS

PROJECT ....

CREATED FOR ....

DATE STARTED .... DATE COMPLETED ....

ITEM .... QTY ....

PRICE .... DEPOSIT PAID .... BALANCE PAID ....

PATTERN USED ....

SUPPLIES NEEDED ....

SKETCH / PHOTO

NOTES

....
....
....
....
....
....
....

Sewing Log Book

DETAILS

PROJECT ....

CREATED FOR ....

DATE STARTED .... DATE COMPLETED ....

ITEM .... QTY ....

PRICE .... DEPOSIT PAID .... BALANCE PAID ....

PATTERN USED ....

SUPPLIES NEEDED ....

SKETCH / PHOTO

NOTES

....
....
....
....
....
....
....
....

Sewing Log Book

DETAILS

PROJECT ....
CREATED FOR ....
DATE STARTED .... DATE COMPLETED ....
ITEM .... QTY ....
PRICE .... DEPOSIT PAID .... BALANCE PAID ....
PATTERN USED ....
SUPPLIES NEEDED ....

SKETCH / PHOTO

NOTES

....
....
....
....
....
....
....

Sewing Log Book

DETAILS

PROJECT ....
CREATED FOR ....
DATE STARTED .... **DATE COMPLETED** ....
ITEM .... **QTY** ....
PRICE .... **DEPOSIT PAID** .... **BALANCE PAID** ....
PATTERN USED ....
SUPPLIES NEEDED ....

SKETCH / PHOTO

NOTES

....
....
....
....
....
....
....

Sewing Log Book

DETAILS

PROJECT ....
CREATED FOR ....
DATE STARTED .... **DATE COMPLETED** ....
ITEM .... **QTY** ....
PRICE .... **DEPOSIT PAID** .... **BALANCE PAID** ....
PATTERN USED ....
SUPPLIES NEEDED ....

SKETCH / PHOTO

NOTES

....
....
....
....
....
....
....

Sewing Log Book

DETAILS

PROJECT ....

CREATED FOR ....

DATE STARTED .... DATE COMPLETED ....

ITEM .... QTY ....

PRICE .... DEPOSIT PAID .... BALANCE PAID ....

PATTERN USED ....

SUPPLIES NEEDED ....

SKETCH / PHOTO

NOTES

....
....
....
....
....
....
....

Sewing Log Book

DETAILS

PROJECT ....
CREATED FOR ....
DATE STARTED .... DATE COMPLETED ....
ITEM .... QTY ....
PRICE .... DEPOSIT PAID .... BALANCE PAID ....
PATTERN USED ....
SUPPLIES NEEDED ....

SKETCH / PHOTO

NOTES

....
....
....
....
....
....
....

Sewing Log Book

DETAILS

PROJECT ....
CREATED FOR ....
DATE STARTED .... **DATE COMPLETED** ....
ITEM .... **QTY** ....
PRICE .... **DEPOSIT PAID** .... **BALANCE PAID** ....
PATTERN USED ....
SUPPLIES NEEDED ....

SKETCH / PHOTO

NOTES

....
....
....
....
....
....
....

Sewing Log Book

DETAILS

PROJECT ....
CREATED FOR ....
DATE STARTED .... **DATE COMPLETED** ....
ITEM .... **QTY** ....
PRICE .... **DEPOSIT PAID** .... **BALANCE PAID** ....
PATTERN USED ....
SUPPLIES NEEDED ....

SKETCH / PHOTO

NOTES

....
....
....
....
....
....
....

Sewing Log Book

DETAILS

PROJECT ....
CREATED FOR ....
DATE STARTED .... DATE COMPLETED ....
ITEM .... QTY ....
PRICE .... DEPOSIT PAID .... BALANCE PAID ....
PATTERN USED ....
SUPPLIES NEEDED ....

SKETCH / PHOTO

NOTES

....
....
....
....
....
....
....

Sewing Log Book

DETAILS

PROJECT ....

CREATED FOR ....

DATE STARTED .... **DATE COMPLETED** ....

ITEM .... **QTY** ....

PRICE .... **DEPOSIT PAID** .... **BALANCE PAID** ....

PATTERN USED ....

SUPPLIES NEEDED ....

SKETCH / PHOTO

NOTES

....
....
....
....
....
....
....

Sewing Log Book

DETAILS

PROJECT ....
CREATED FOR ....
DATE STARTED .... **DATE COMPLETED** ....
ITEM .... **QTY** ....
PRICE .... **DEPOSIT PAID** .... **BALANCE PAID** ....
PATTERN USED ....
SUPPLIES NEEDED ....

SKETCH / PHOTO

NOTES

....
....
....
....
....
....
....
....

Sewing Log Book

DETAILS

PROJECT ....
CREATED FOR ....
DATE STARTED .... **DATE COMPLETED** ....
ITEM .... **QTY** ....
PRICE .... **DEPOSIT PAID** .... **BALANCE PAID** ....
PATTERN USED ....
SUPPLIES NEEDED ....

SKETCH / PHOTO

NOTES

....
....
....
....
....
....
....

Sewing Log Book

DETAILS

PROJECT ....

CREATED FOR ....

DATE STARTED .... DATE COMPLETED ....

ITEM .... QTY ....

PRICE .... DEPOSIT PAID .... BALANCE PAID ....

PATTERN USED ....

SUPPLIES NEEDED ....

SKETCH / PHOTO

NOTES

....
....
....
....
....
....
....
....

Sewing Log Book

DETAILS

PROJECT ....
CREATED FOR ....
DATE STARTED .... **DATE COMPLETED** ....
ITEM .... **QTY** ....
PRICE .... **DEPOSIT PAID** .... **BALANCE PAID** ....
PATTERN USED ....
SUPPLIES NEEDED ....

SKETCH / PHOTO

NOTES

....
....
....
....
....
....
....

Sewing Log Book

DETAILS

PROJECT ....

CREATED FOR ....

DATE STARTED .... DATE COMPLETED ....

ITEM .... QTY ....

PRICE .... DEPOSIT PAID .... BALANCE PAID ....

PATTERN USED ....

SUPPLIES NEEDED ....

SKETCH / PHOTO

NOTES

....
....
....
....
....
....
....

Sewing Log Book

DETAILS

PROJECT ....
CREATED FOR ....
DATE STARTED .... **DATE COMPLETED** ....
ITEM .... **QTY** ....
PRICE .... **DEPOSIT PAID** .... **BALANCE PAID** ....
PATTERN USED ....
SUPPLIES NEEDED ....

SKETCH / PHOTO

NOTES

....
....
....
....
....
....
....

Sewing Log Book

DETAILS

PROJECT ....
CREATED FOR ....
DATE STARTED .... DATE COMPLETED ....
ITEM .... QTY ....
PRICE .... DEPOSIT PAID .... BALANCE PAID ....
PATTERN USED ....
SUPPLIES NEEDED ....

SKETCH / PHOTO

NOTES

....
....
....
....
....
....
....
....

Sewing Log Book

DETAILS

PROJECT ....

CREATED FOR ....

DATE STARTED .... **DATE COMPLETED** ....

ITEM .... **QTY** ....

PRICE .... **DEPOSIT PAID** .... **BALANCE PAID** ....

PATTERN USED ....

SUPPLIES NEEDED ....

SKETCH / PHOTO

NOTES

....
....
....
....
....
....
....

Sewing Log Book

DETAILS

PROJECT ....
CREATED FOR ....
DATE STARTED .... DATE COMPLETED ....
ITEM .... QTY ....
PRICE .... DEPOSIT PAID .... BALANCE PAID ....
PATTERN USED ....
SUPPLIES NEEDED ....

SKETCH / PHOTO

NOTES

....
....
....
....
....
....
....

Sewing Log Book

DETAILS

PROJECT ....

CREATED FOR ....

DATE STARTED .... DATE COMPLETED ....

ITEM .... QTY ....

PRICE .... DEPOSIT PAID .... BALANCE PAID ....

PATTERN USED ....

SUPPLIES NEEDED ....

SKETCH / PHOTO

NOTES

....
....
....
....
....
....
....

Sewing Log Book

DETAILS

PROJECT ....

CREATED FOR ....

DATE STARTED .... DATE COMPLETED ....

ITEM .... QTY ....

PRICE .... DEPOSIT PAID .... BALANCE PAID ....

PATTERN USED ....

SUPPLIES NEEDED ....

SKETCH / PHOTO

NOTES

....
....
....
....
....
....
....
....

Sewing Log Book

DETAILS

PROJECT ....
CREATED FOR ....
DATE STARTED .... **DATE COMPLETED** ....
ITEM .... **QTY** ....
PRICE .... **DEPOSIT PAID** .... **BALANCE PAID** ....
PATTERN USED ....
SUPPLIES NEEDED ....

SKETCH / PHOTO

NOTES

....
....
....
....
....
....
....
....

Sewing Log Book

DETAILS

PROJECT ....
CREATED FOR ....
DATE STARTED .... DATE COMPLETED ....
ITEM .... QTY ....
PRICE .... DEPOSIT PAID .... BALANCE PAID ....
PATTERN USED ....
SUPPLIES NEEDED ....

SKETCH / PHOTO

NOTES

....
....
....
....
....
....
....
....

Sewing Log Book

DETAILS

PROJECT ....
CREATED FOR ....
DATE STARTED .... **DATE COMPLETED** ....
ITEM .... **QTY** ....
PRICE .... **DEPOSIT PAID** .... **BALANCE PAID** ....
PATTERN USED ....
SUPPLIES NEEDED ....

SKETCH / PHOTO

NOTES

....
....
....
....
....
....
....

Sewing Log Book

DETAILS

PROJECT ....

CREATED FOR ....

DATE STARTED .... DATE COMPLETED ....

ITEM .... QTY ....

PRICE .... DEPOSIT PAID .... BALANCE PAID ....

PATTERN USED ....

SUPPLIES NEEDED ....

SKETCH / PHOTO

NOTES

....
....
....
....
....
....
....
....

Sewing Log Book

DETAILS

PROJECT ....
CREATED FOR ....
DATE STARTED .... **DATE COMPLETED** ....
ITEM .... **QTY** ....
PRICE .... **DEPOSIT PAID** .... **BALANCE PAID** ....
PATTERN USED ....
SUPPLIES NEEDED ....

SKETCH / PHOTO

NOTES

....
....
....
....
....
....
....

Sewing Log Book

DETAILS

PROJECT ....
CREATED FOR ....
DATE STARTED .... DATE COMPLETED ....
ITEM .... QTY ....
PRICE .... DEPOSIT PAID .... BALANCE PAID ....
PATTERN USED ....
SUPPLIES NEEDED ....

SKETCH / PHOTO

NOTES

....
....
....
....
....
....
....
....

Sewing Log Book

DETAILS

PROJECT ....

CREATED FOR ....

DATE STARTED .... DATE COMPLETED ....

ITEM .... QTY ....

PRICE .... DEPOSIT PAID .... BALANCE PAID ....

PATTERN USED ....

SUPPLIES NEEDED ....

SKETCH / PHOTO

NOTES

....
....
....
....
....
....
....
....

Sewing Log Book

DETAILS

PROJECT ....
CREATED FOR ....
DATE STARTED .... DATE COMPLETED ....
ITEM .... QTY ....
PRICE .... DEPOSIT PAID .... BALANCE PAID ....
PATTERN USED ....
SUPPLIES NEEDED ....

SKETCH / PHOTO

NOTES

....
....
....
....
....
....
....
....

Sewing Log Book

DETAILS

PROJECT ....
CREATED FOR ....
DATE STARTED .... **DATE COMPLETED** ....
ITEM .... **QTY** ....
PRICE .... **DEPOSIT PAID** .... **BALANCE PAID** ....
PATTERN USED ....
SUPPLIES NEEDED ....

SKETCH / PHOTO

NOTES

....
....
....
....
....
....
....

Sewing Log Book

DETAILS

PROJECT ....
CREATED FOR ....
DATE STARTED .... **DATE COMPLETED** ....
ITEM .... **QTY** ....
PRICE .... **DEPOSIT PAID** .... **BALANCE PAID** ....
PATTERN USED ....
SUPPLIES NEEDED ....

SKETCH / PHOTO

NOTES

....
....
....
....
....
....
....
....

Sewing Log Book

DETAILS

PROJECT ....
CREATED FOR ....
DATE STARTED .... **DATE COMPLETED** ....
ITEM .... **QTY** ....
PRICE .... **DEPOSIT PAID** .... **BALANCE PAID** ....
PATTERN USED ....
SUPPLIES NEEDED ....

SKETCH / PHOTO

NOTES

....
....
....
....
....
....
....
....

Sewing Log Book

DETAILS

PROJECT ....
CREATED FOR ....
DATE STARTED .... DATE COMPLETED ....
ITEM .... QTY ....
PRICE .... DEPOSIT PAID .... BALANCE PAID ....
PATTERN USED ....
SUPPLIES NEEDED ....

SKETCH / PHOTO

NOTES

....
....
....
....
....
....
....
....

Sewing Log Book

DETAILS

PROJECT ....
CREATED FOR ....
DATE STARTED .... **DATE COMPLETED** ....
ITEM .... **QTY** ....
PRICE .... **DEPOSIT PAID** .... **BALANCE PAID** ....
PATTERN USED ....
SUPPLIES NEEDED ....

SKETCH / PHOTO

NOTES

....
....
....
....
....
....
....
....

Sewing Log Book

DETAILS

PROJECT ....
CREATED FOR ....
DATE STARTED .... **DATE COMPLETED** ....
ITEM .... **QTY** ....
PRICE .... **DEPOSIT PAID** .... **BALANCE PAID** ....
PATTERN USED ....
SUPPLIES NEEDED ....

SKETCH / PHOTO

NOTES

....
....
....
....
....
....
....
....

Sewing Log Book

DETAILS

PROJECT ....

CREATED FOR ....

DATE STARTED .... **DATE COMPLETED** ....

ITEM .... **QTY** ....

PRICE .... **DEPOSIT PAID** .... **BALANCE PAID** ....

PATTERN USED ....

SUPPLIES NEEDED ....

SKETCH / PHOTO

NOTES

....
....
....
....
....
....
....
....

Sewing Log Book

DETAILS

PROJECT ....
CREATED FOR ....
DATE STARTED .... **DATE COMPLETED** ....
ITEM .... **QTY** ....
PRICE .... **DEPOSIT PAID** .... **BALANCE PAID** ....
PATTERN USED ....
SUPPLIES NEEDED ....

SKETCH / PHOTO

NOTES

....
....
....
....
....
....
....

Sewing Log Book

DETAILS

PROJECT ....
CREATED FOR ....
DATE STARTED .... **DATE COMPLETED** ....
ITEM .... **QTY** ....
PRICE .... **DEPOSIT PAID** .... **BALANCE PAID** ....
PATTERN USED ....
SUPPLIES NEEDED ....

SKETCH / PHOTO

NOTES

....
....
....
....
....
....
....

Sewing Log Book

DETAILS

PROJECT ....
CREATED FOR ....
DATE STARTED .... **DATE COMPLETED** ....
ITEM .... **QTY** ....
PRICE .... **DEPOSIT PAID** .... **BALANCE PAID** ....
PATTERN USED ....
SUPPLIES NEEDED ....

SKETCH / PHOTO

NOTES

....
....
....
....
....
....
....

Sewing Log Book

DETAILS

PROJECT ....
CREATED FOR ....
DATE STARTED .... **DATE COMPLETED** ....
ITEM .... **QTY** ....
PRICE .... **DEPOSIT PAID** .... **BALANCE PAID** ....
PATTERN USED ....
SUPPLIES NEEDED ....

SKETCH / PHOTO

NOTES

....
....
....
....
....
....
....

Sewing Log Book

DETAILS

PROJECT ....
CREATED FOR ....
DATE STARTED .... **DATE COMPLETED** ....
ITEM .... **QTY** ....
PRICE .... **DEPOSIT PAID** .... **BALANCE PAID** ....
PATTERN USED ....
SUPPLIES NEEDED ....

SKETCH / PHOTO

NOTES

....
....
....
....
....
....
....
....

Sewing Log Book

DETAILS

PROJECT ....

CREATED FOR ....

DATE STARTED .... DATE COMPLETED ....

ITEM .... QTY ....

PRICE .... DEPOSIT PAID .... BALANCE PAID ....

PATTERN USED ....

SUPPLIES NEEDED ....

SKETCH / PHOTO

NOTES

....
....
....
....
....
....
....

Sewing Log Book

DETAILS

PROJECT ....
CREATED FOR ....
DATE STARTED .... DATE COMPLETED ....
ITEM .... QTY ....
PRICE .... DEPOSIT PAID .... BALANCE PAID ....
PATTERN USED ....
SUPPLIES NEEDED ....

SKETCH / PHOTO

NOTES

....
....
....
....
....
....
....
....

Sewing Log Book

DETAILS

PROJECT ....

CREATED FOR ....

DATE STARTED .... DATE COMPLETED ....

ITEM .... QTY ....

PRICE .... DEPOSIT PAID .... BALANCE PAID ....

PATTERN USED ....

SUPPLIES NEEDED ....

SKETCH / PHOTO

NOTES

....
....
....
....
....
....
....

Sewing Log Book

DETAILS

PROJECT ....
CREATED FOR ....
DATE STARTED .... **DATE COMPLETED** ....
ITEM .... **QTY** ....
PRICE .... **DEPOSIT PAID** .... **BALANCE PAID** ....
PATTERN USED ....
SUPPLIES NEEDED ....

SKETCH / PHOTO

NOTES

....
....
....
....
....
....
....

Sewing Log Book

DETAILS

PROJECT ....

CREATED FOR ....

DATE STARTED .... DATE COMPLETED ....

ITEM .... QTY ....

PRICE .... DEPOSIT PAID .... BALANCE PAID ....

PATTERN USED ....

SUPPLIES NEEDED ....

SKETCH / PHOTO

NOTES

....
....
....
....
....
....
....

Sewing Log Book

DETAILS

PROJECT ....
CREATED FOR ....
DATE STARTED .... DATE COMPLETED ....
ITEM .... QTY ....
PRICE .... DEPOSIT PAID .... BALANCE PAID ....
PATTERN USED ....
SUPPLIES NEEDED ....

SKETCH / PHOTO

NOTES

....
....
....
....
....
....
....
....

Sewing Log Book

DETAILS

PROJECT ....
CREATED FOR ....
DATE STARTED .... **DATE COMPLETED** ....
ITEM .... **QTY** ....
PRICE .... **DEPOSIT PAID** .... **BALANCE PAID** ....
PATTERN USED ....
SUPPLIES NEEDED ....

SKETCH / PHOTO

NOTES

....
....
....
....
....
....
....

Sewing Log Book

DETAILS

PROJECT ....
CREATED FOR ....
DATE STARTED .... **DATE COMPLETED** ....
ITEM .... **QTY** ....
PRICE .... **DEPOSIT PAID** .... **BALANCE PAID** ....
PATTERN USED ....
SUPPLIES NEEDED ....

SKETCH / PHOTO

NOTES

....
....
....
....
....
....
....
....

Sewing Log Book

DETAILS

PROJECT ....
CREATED FOR ....
DATE STARTED .... **DATE COMPLETED** ....
ITEM .... **QTY** ....
PRICE .... **DEPOSIT PAID** .... **BALANCE PAID** ....
PATTERN USED ....
SUPPLIES NEEDED ....

SKETCH / PHOTO

NOTES

....
....
....
....
....
....
....

Sewing Log Book

DETAILS

PROJECT ....

CREATED FOR ....

DATE STARTED .... DATE COMPLETED ....

ITEM .... QTY ....

PRICE .... DEPOSIT PAID .... BALANCE PAID ....

PATTERN USED ....

SUPPLIES NEEDED ....

SKETCH / PHOTO

NOTES

....
....
....
....
....
....
....
....

Sewing Log Book

DETAILS

PROJECT ....
CREATED FOR ....
DATE STARTED .... **DATE COMPLETED** ....
ITEM .... **QTY** ....
PRICE .... **DEPOSIT PAID** .... **BALANCE PAID** ....
PATTERN USED ....
SUPPLIES NEEDED ....

SKETCH / PHOTO

NOTES

....
....
....
....
....
....
....
....

Sewing Log Book

DETAILS

PROJECT ....
CREATED FOR ....
DATE STARTED .... **DATE COMPLETED** ....
ITEM .... **QTY** ....
PRICE .... **DEPOSIT PAID** .... **BALANCE PAID** ....
PATTERN USED ....
SUPPLIES NEEDED ....

SKETCH / PHOTO

NOTES

....
....
....
....
....
....
....
....

Sewing Log Book

DETAILS

PROJECT ....
CREATED FOR ....
DATE STARTED .... **DATE COMPLETED** ....
ITEM .... **QTY** ....
PRICE .... **DEPOSIT PAID** .... **BALANCE PAID** ....
PATTERN USED ....
SUPPLIES NEEDED ....

SKETCH / PHOTO

NOTES

....
....
....
....
....
....
....

Sewing Log Book

DETAILS

PROJECT ....
CREATED FOR ....
DATE STARTED .... **DATE COMPLETED** ....
ITEM .... **QTY** ....
PRICE .... **DEPOSIT PAID** .... **BALANCE PAID** ....
PATTERN USED ....
SUPPLIES NEEDED ....

SKETCH / PHOTO

NOTES

....
....
....
....
....
....
....
....

Sewing Log Book

DETAILS

PROJECT ....
CREATED FOR ....
DATE STARTED .... DATE COMPLETED ....
ITEM .... QTY ....
PRICE .... DEPOSIT PAID .... BALANCE PAID ....
PATTERN USED ....
SUPPLIES NEEDED ....

SKETCH / PHOTO

NOTES

....
....
....
....
....
....
....

Sewing Log Book

DETAILS

PROJECT ....
CREATED FOR ....
DATE STARTED .... **DATE COMPLETED** ....
ITEM .... **QTY** ....
PRICE .... **DEPOSIT PAID** .... **BALANCE PAID** ....
PATTERN USED ....
SUPPLIES NEEDED ....

SKETCH / PHOTO

NOTES

....
....
....
....
....
....
....

Sewing Log Book

DETAILS

PROJECT ....
CREATED FOR ....
DATE STARTED .... DATE COMPLETED ....
ITEM .... QTY ....
PRICE .... DEPOSIT PAID .... BALANCE PAID ....
PATTERN USED ....
SUPPLIES NEEDED ....

SKETCH / PHOTO

NOTES

....
....
....
....
....
....
....

Sewing Log Book

DETAILS

PROJECT ....
CREATED FOR ....
DATE STARTED .... DATE COMPLETED ....
ITEM .... QTY ....
PRICE .... DEPOSIT PAID .... BALANCE PAID ....
PATTERN USED ....
SUPPLIES NEEDED ....

SKETCH / PHOTO

NOTES

....
....
....
....
....
....
....
....

Sewing Log Book

DETAILS

PROJECT ....

CREATED FOR ....

DATE STARTED .... DATE COMPLETED ....

ITEM .... QTY ....

PRICE .... DEPOSIT PAID .... BALANCE PAID ....

PATTERN USED ....

SUPPLIES NEEDED ....

SKETCH / PHOTO

NOTES

....
....
....
....
....
....
....

Sewing Log Book

DETAILS

PROJECT ....
CREATED FOR ....
DATE STARTED .... **DATE COMPLETED** ....
ITEM .... **QTY** ....
PRICE .... **DEPOSIT PAID** .... **BALANCE PAID** ....
PATTERN USED ....
SUPPLIES NEEDED ....

SKETCH / PHOTO

NOTES

....
....
....
....
....
....
....

Sewing Log Book

DETAILS

PROJECT ....

CREATED FOR ....

DATE STARTED .... **DATE COMPLETED** ....

ITEM .... **QTY** ....

PRICE .... **DEPOSIT PAID** .... **BALANCE PAID** ....

PATTERN USED ....

SUPPLIES NEEDED ....

SKETCH / PHOTO

NOTES

....
....
....
....
....
....
....

Sewing Log Book

DETAILS

- **PROJECT** ....
- **CREATED FOR** ....
- **DATE STARTED** .... **DATE COMPLETED** ....
- **ITEM** .... **QTY** ....
- **PRICE** .... **DEPOSIT PAID** .... **BALANCE PAID** ....
- **PATTERN USED** ....
- **SUPPLIES NEEDED** ....

SKETCH / PHOTO

NOTES

....
....
....
....
....
....
....
....

Sewing Log Book

DETAILS

PROJECT ....
CREATED FOR ....
DATE STARTED .... **DATE COMPLETED** ....
ITEM .... **QTY** ....
PRICE .... **DEPOSIT PAID** .... **BALANCE PAID** ....
PATTERN USED ....
SUPPLIES NEEDED ....

SKETCH / PHOTO

NOTES

....
....
....
....
....
....
....
....

Sewing Log Book

DETAILS

PROJECT ....
CREATED FOR ....
DATE STARTED .... **DATE COMPLETED** ....
ITEM .... **QTY** ....
PRICE .... **DEPOSIT PAID** .... **BALANCE PAID** ....
PATTERN USED ....
SUPPLIES NEEDED ....

SKETCH / PHOTO

NOTES

....
....
....
....
....
....
....
....

Sewing Log Book

DETAILS

PROJECT ....
CREATED FOR ....
DATE STARTED .... DATE COMPLETED ....
ITEM .... QTY ....
PRICE .... DEPOSIT PAID .... BALANCE PAID ....
PATTERN USED ....
SUPPLIES NEEDED ....

SKETCH / PHOTO

NOTES

....
....
....
....
....
....
....

Sewing Log Book

DETAILS

PROJECT ....
CREATED FOR ....
DATE STARTED .... **DATE COMPLETED** ....
ITEM .... **QTY** ....
PRICE .... **DEPOSIT PAID** .... **BALANCE PAID** ....
PATTERN USED ....
SUPPLIES NEEDED ....

SKETCH / PHOTO

NOTES

....
....
....
....
....
....
....
....

Sewing Log Book

DETAILS

PROJECT ....

CREATED FOR ....

DATE STARTED .... DATE COMPLETED ....

ITEM .... QTY ....

PRICE .... DEPOSIT PAID .... BALANCE PAID ....

PATTERN USED ....

SUPPLIES NEEDED ....

SKETCH / PHOTO

NOTES

....
....
....
....
....
....
....

Sewing Log Book

DETAILS

PROJECT ....

CREATED FOR ....

DATE STARTED .... **DATE COMPLETED** ....

ITEM .... **QTY** ....

PRICE .... **DEPOSIT PAID** .... **BALANCE PAID** ....

PATTERN USED ....

SUPPLIES NEEDED ....

SKETCH / PHOTO

NOTES

....
....
....
....
....
....
....

Sewing Log Book

DETAILS

PROJECT ....
CREATED FOR ....
DATE STARTED .... **DATE COMPLETED** ....
ITEM .... **QTY** ....
PRICE .... **DEPOSIT PAID** .... **BALANCE PAID** ....
PATTERN USED ....
SUPPLIES NEEDED ....

SKETCH / PHOTO

NOTES

....
....
....
....
....
....
....

Sewing Log Book

DETAILS

PROJECT ....
CREATED FOR ....
DATE STARTED .... **DATE COMPLETED** ....
ITEM .... **QTY** ....
PRICE .... **DEPOSIT PAID** .... **BALANCE PAID** ....
PATTERN USED ....
SUPPLIES NEEDED ....

SKETCH / PHOTO

NOTES

....
....
....
....
....
....
....
....

Sewing Log Book

DETAILS

PROJECT ....
CREATED FOR ....
DATE STARTED .... DATE COMPLETED ....
ITEM .... QTY ....
PRICE .... DEPOSIT PAID .... BALANCE PAID ....
PATTERN USED ....
SUPPLIES NEEDED ....

SKETCH / PHOTO

NOTES

....
....
....
....
....
....
....
....

Sewing Log Book

DETAILS

PROJECT ....

CREATED FOR ....

DATE STARTED .... DATE COMPLETED ....

ITEM .... QTY ....

PRICE .... DEPOSIT PAID .... BALANCE PAID ....

PATTERN USED ....

SUPPLIES NEEDED ....

SKETCH / PHOTO

NOTES

....
....
....
....
....
....
....
....

Sewing Log Book

DETAILS

PROJECT ....
CREATED FOR ....
DATE STARTED .... **DATE COMPLETED** ....
ITEM .... **QTY** ....
PRICE .... **DEPOSIT PAID** .... **BALANCE PAID** ....
PATTERN USED ....
SUPPLIES NEEDED ....

SKETCH / PHOTO

NOTES

....
....
....
....
....
....
....

Sewing Log Book

DETAILS

PROJECT ....
CREATED FOR ....
DATE STARTED .... **DATE COMPLETED** ....
ITEM .... **QTY** ....
PRICE .... **DEPOSIT PAID** .... **BALANCE PAID** ....
PATTERN USED ....
SUPPLIES NEEDED ....

SKETCH / PHOTO

NOTES

....
....
....
....
....
....
....

Sewing Log Book

DETAILS

PROJECT ....
CREATED FOR ....
DATE STARTED .... **DATE COMPLETED** ....
ITEM .... **QTY** ....
PRICE .... **DEPOSIT PAID** .... **BALANCE PAID** ....
PATTERN USED ....
SUPPLIES NEEDED ....

SKETCH / PHOTO

NOTES

....
....
....
....
....
....
....
....

Sewing Log Book

DETAILS

PROJECT ....
CREATED FOR ....
DATE STARTED .... **DATE COMPLETED** ....
ITEM .... **QTY** ....
PRICE .... **DEPOSIT PAID** .... **BALANCE PAID** ....
PATTERN USED ....
SUPPLIES NEEDED ....

SKETCH / PHOTO

NOTES

....
....
....
....
....
....
....
....

Sewing Log Book

DETAILS

PROJECT ....

CREATED FOR ....

DATE STARTED .... **DATE COMPLETED** ....

ITEM .... **QTY** ....

PRICE .... **DEPOSIT PAID** .... **BALANCE PAID** ....

PATTERN USED ....

SUPPLIES NEEDED ....

SKETCH / PHOTO

NOTES

....
....
....
....
....
....
....

Sewing Log Book

DETAILS

PROJECT ....
CREATED FOR ....
DATE STARTED .... **DATE COMPLETED** ....
ITEM .... **QTY** ....
PRICE .... **DEPOSIT PAID** .... **BALANCE PAID** ....
PATTERN USED ....
SUPPLIES NEEDED ....

SKETCH / PHOTO

NOTES

....
....
....
....
....
....
....
....

Sewing Log Book

DETAILS

PROJECT ....

CREATED FOR ....

DATE STARTED .... DATE COMPLETED ....

ITEM .... QTY ....

PRICE .... DEPOSIT PAID .... BALANCE PAID ....

PATTERN USED ....

SUPPLIES NEEDED ....

SKETCH / PHOTO

NOTES

....
....
....
....
....
....
....

Sewing Log Book

DETAILS

PROJECT ....

CREATED FOR ....

DATE STARTED .... **DATE COMPLETED** ....

ITEM .... **QTY** ....

PRICE .... **DEPOSIT PAID** .... **BALANCE PAID** ....

PATTERN USED ....

SUPPLIES NEEDED ....

SKETCH / PHOTO

NOTES

....
....
....
....
....
....
....

Sewing Log Book

DETAILS

PROJECT ....
CREATED FOR ....
DATE STARTED .... **DATE COMPLETED** ....
ITEM .... **QTY** ....
PRICE .... **DEPOSIT PAID** .... **BALANCE PAID** ....
PATTERN USED ....
SUPPLIES NEEDED ....

SKETCH / PHOTO

NOTES

....
....
....
....
....
....
....

Sewing Log Book

DETAILS

PROJECT ....
CREATED FOR ....
DATE STARTED .... **DATE COMPLETED** ....
ITEM .... **QTY** ....
PRICE .... **DEPOSIT PAID** .... **BALANCE PAID** ....
PATTERN USED ....
SUPPLIES NEEDED ....

SKETCH / PHOTO

NOTES

....
....
....
....
....
....
....
....

Sewing Log Book

DETAILS

PROJECT ....
CREATED FOR ....
DATE STARTED .... DATE COMPLETED ....
ITEM .... QTY ....
PRICE .... DEPOSIT PAID .... BALANCE PAID ....
PATTERN USED ....
SUPPLIES NEEDED ....

SKETCH / PHOTO

NOTES

....
....
....
....
....
....
....

Sewing Log Book

DETAILS

PROJECT ....
CREATED FOR ....
DATE STARTED .... DATE COMPLETED ....
ITEM .... QTY ....
PRICE .... DEPOSIT PAID .... BALANCE PAID ....
PATTERN USED ....
SUPPLIES NEEDED ....

SKETCH / PHOTO

NOTES

....
....
....
....
....
....
....

Sewing Log Book

DETAILS

PROJECT ....
CREATED FOR ....
DATE STARTED .... **DATE COMPLETED** ....
ITEM .... **QTY** ....
PRICE .... **DEPOSIT PAID** .... **BALANCE PAID** ....
PATTERN USED ....
SUPPLIES NEEDED ....

SKETCH / PHOTO

NOTES

....
....
....
....
....
....
....

Sewing Log Book

DETAILS

PROJECT ....

CREATED FOR ....

DATE STARTED .... DATE COMPLETED ....

ITEM .... QTY ....

PRICE .... DEPOSIT PAID .... BALANCE PAID ....

PATTERN USED ....

SUPPLIES NEEDED ....

SKETCH / PHOTO

NOTES

....
....
....
....
....
....
....

Sewing Log Book

DETAILS

PROJECT ....
CREATED FOR ....
DATE STARTED .... **DATE COMPLETED** ....
ITEM .... **QTY** ....
PRICE .... **DEPOSIT PAID** .... **BALANCE PAID** ....
PATTERN USED ....
SUPPLIES NEEDED ....

SKETCH / PHOTO

NOTES

....
....
....
....
....
....
....
....

Sewing Log Book

DETAILS

PROJECT ....
CREATED FOR ....
DATE STARTED .... **DATE COMPLETED** ....
ITEM .... **QTY** ....
PRICE .... **DEPOSIT PAID** .... **BALANCE PAID** ....
PATTERN USED ....
SUPPLIES NEEDED ....

SKETCH / PHOTO

NOTES

....
....
....
....
....
....
....
....

Sewing Log Book

DETAILS

PROJECT ....
CREATED FOR ....
DATE STARTED .... **DATE COMPLETED** ....
ITEM .... **QTY** ....
PRICE .... **DEPOSIT PAID** .... **BALANCE PAID** ....
PATTERN USED ....
SUPPLIES NEEDED ....

SKETCH / PHOTO

NOTES

....
....
....
....
....
....
....

Sewing Log Book

DETAILS

PROJECT ....
CREATED FOR ....
DATE STARTED .... **DATE COMPLETED** ....
ITEM .... **QTY** ....
PRICE .... **DEPOSIT PAID** .... **BALANCE PAID** ....
PATTERN USED ....
SUPPLIES NEEDED ....

SKETCH / PHOTO

NOTES

....
....
....
....
....
....
....
....

Sewing Log Book

DETAILS

PROJECT ....
CREATED FOR ....
DATE STARTED .... **DATE COMPLETED** ....
ITEM .... **QTY** ....
PRICE .... **DEPOSIT PAID** .... **BALANCE PAID** ....
PATTERN USED ....
SUPPLIES NEEDED ....

SKETCH / PHOTO

NOTES

....
....
....
....
....
....

Sewing Log Book

DETAILS

PROJECT ....

CREATED FOR ....

DATE STARTED .... DATE COMPLETED ....

ITEM .... QTY ....

PRICE .... DEPOSIT PAID .... BALANCE PAID ....

PATTERN USED ....

SUPPLIES NEEDED ....

SKETCH / PHOTO

NOTES

....
....
....
....
....
....
....

Sewing Log Book

DETAILS

PROJECT ....
CREATED FOR ....
DATE STARTED .... **DATE COMPLETED** ....
ITEM .... **QTY** ....
PRICE .... **DEPOSIT PAID** .... **BALANCE PAID** ....
PATTERN USED ....
SUPPLIES NEEDED ....

SKETCH / PHOTO

NOTES

....
....
....
....
....
....
....

Sewing Log Book

DETAILS

PROJECT ....
CREATED FOR ....
DATE STARTED .... **DATE COMPLETED** ....
ITEM .... **QTY** ....
PRICE .... **DEPOSIT PAID** .... **BALANCE PAID** ....
PATTERN USED ....
SUPPLIES NEEDED ....

SKETCH / PHOTO

NOTES

....
....
....
....
....
....
....
....

Sewing Log Book

DETAILS

PROJECT ....
CREATED FOR ....
DATE STARTED .... DATE COMPLETED ....
ITEM .... QTY ....
PRICE .... DEPOSIT PAID .... BALANCE PAID ....
PATTERN USED ....
SUPPLIES NEEDED ....

SKETCH / PHOTO

NOTES

....
....
....
....
....
....
....

Sewing Log Book

DETAILS

PROJECT ....

CREATED FOR ....

DATE STARTED .... **DATE COMPLETED** ....

ITEM .... **QTY** ....

PRICE .... **DEPOSIT PAID** .... **BALANCE PAID** ....

PATTERN USED ....

SUPPLIES NEEDED ....

SKETCH / PHOTO

NOTES

....
....
....
....
....
....
....
....

Sewing Log Book

DETAILS

PROJECT ....

CREATED FOR ....

DATE STARTED .... **DATE COMPLETED** ....

ITEM .... **QTY** ....

PRICE .... **DEPOSIT PAID** .... **BALANCE PAID** ....

PATTERN USED ....

SUPPLIES NEEDED ....

SKETCH / PHOTO

NOTES

....
....
....
....
....
....
....

Sewing Log Book

DETAILS

PROJECT ....
CREATED FOR ....
DATE STARTED .... **DATE COMPLETED** ....
ITEM .... **QTY** ....
PRICE .... **DEPOSIT PAID** .... **BALANCE PAID** ....
PATTERN USED ....
SUPPLIES NEEDED ....

SKETCH / PHOTO

NOTES

....
....
....
....
....
....
....

Sewing Log Book

DETAILS

PROJECT ....
CREATED FOR ....
DATE STARTED .... **DATE COMPLETED** ....
ITEM .... **QTY** ....
PRICE .... **DEPOSIT PAID** .... **BALANCE PAID** ....
PATTERN USED ....
SUPPLIES NEEDED ....

SKETCH / PHOTO

NOTES

....
....
....
....
....
....
....

Sewing Log Book

DETAILS

PROJECT ....
CREATED FOR ....
DATE STARTED .... **DATE COMPLETED** ....
ITEM .... **QTY** ....
PRICE .... **DEPOSIT PAID** .... **BALANCE PAID** ....
PATTERN USED ....
SUPPLIES NEEDED ....

SKETCH / PHOTO

NOTES

....
....
....
....
....
....
....
....

Sewing Log Book

DETAILS

PROJECT ....
CREATED FOR ....
DATE STARTED .... **DATE COMPLETED** ....
ITEM .... **QTY** ....
PRICE .... **DEPOSIT PAID** .... **BALANCE PAID** ....
PATTERN USED ....
SUPPLIES NEEDED ....

SKETCH / PHOTO

NOTES

....
....
....
....
....
....
....

Sewing Log Book

DETAILS

PROJECT ....
CREATED FOR ....
DATE STARTED .... **DATE COMPLETED** ....
ITEM .... **QTY** ....
PRICE .... **DEPOSIT PAID** .... **BALANCE PAID** ....
PATTERN USED ....
SUPPLIES NEEDED ....

SKETCH / PHOTO

NOTES

....
....
....
....
....
....
....

Sewing Log Book

DETAILS

PROJECT ....
CREATED FOR ....
DATE STARTED .... DATE COMPLETED ....
ITEM .... QTY ....
PRICE .... DEPOSIT PAID .... BALANCE PAID ....
PATTERN USED ....
SUPPLIES NEEDED ....

SKETCH / PHOTO

NOTES

....
....
....
....
....
....
....

Sewing Log Book

DETAILS

PROJECT ....

CREATED FOR ....

DATE STARTED .... DATE COMPLETED ....

ITEM .... QTY ....

PRICE .... DEPOSIT PAID .... BALANCE PAID ....

PATTERN USED ....

SUPPLIES NEEDED ....

SKETCH / PHOTO

NOTES

....
....
....
....
....
....
....
....

Sewing Log Book

DETAILS

PROJECT ....
CREATED FOR ....
DATE STARTED .... **DATE COMPLETED** ....
ITEM .... **QTY** ....
PRICE .... **DEPOSIT PAID** .... **BALANCE PAID** ....
PATTERN USED ....
SUPPLIES NEEDED ....

SKETCH / PHOTO

NOTES

....
....
....
....
....
....
....
....

Sewing Log Book

DETAILS

PROJECT ....

CREATED FOR ....

DATE STARTED .... **DATE COMPLETED** ....

ITEM .... **QTY** ....

PRICE .... **DEPOSIT PAID** .... **BALANCE PAID** ....

PATTERN USED ....

SUPPLIES NEEDED ....

SKETCH / PHOTO

NOTES

....
....
....
....
....
....
....
....

Sewing Log Book

DETAILS

PROJECT ....

CREATED FOR ....

DATE STARTED .... **DATE COMPLETED** ....

ITEM .... **QTY** ....

PRICE .... **DEPOSIT PAID** .... **BALANCE PAID** ....

PATTERN USED ....

SUPPLIES NEEDED ....

SKETCH / PHOTO

NOTES

....
....
....
....
....
....
....

Sewing Log Book

DETAILS

PROJECT ....
CREATED FOR ....
DATE STARTED .... **DATE COMPLETED** ....
ITEM .... **QTY** ....
PRICE .... **DEPOSIT PAID** .... **BALANCE PAID** ....
PATTERN USED ....
SUPPLIES NEEDED ....

SKETCH / PHOTO

NOTES

....
....
....
....
....
....
....
....

Sewing Log Book

DETAILS

PROJECT ....

CREATED FOR ....

DATE STARTED .... DATE COMPLETED ....

ITEM .... QTY ....

PRICE .... DEPOSIT PAID .... BALANCE PAID ....

PATTERN USED ....

SUPPLIES NEEDED ....

SKETCH / PHOTO

NOTES

....
....
....
....
....
....
....
....

www.ingramcontent.com/pod-product-compliance
Lightning Source LLC
Chambersburg PA
CBHW050257120526
44590CB00016B/2391